F F RECIPES

compiled by
Brunella Ponzo

*with illustrations
of Italian life
and landscape*

SALMON

Index

Cover pictures front: Figures on a terrace in Capri *by Robert Alott*
back: The Grand Canal, Venice *by Rubens Santoro*
title page: A glimpse of Lake Como, Lombardy

Printed and published by Dorrigo, Manchester, England © Copyright

Introduction

This book should give you the basics for preparing a good dish of fresh pasta quickly and wherever you may be. Portions are calculated for 4 to 6 persons. You can alter them proportionately either for an intimate meal or for a larger number of guests.

"Dry pasta" and "filled pasta" are the two major categories of the endless world of pasta. Amongst the former are tagliatelle, tagliolini, maltagliati, linguine, fettuccine, pizzoccheri, pappardelle and lasagne, the difference between them being simply a matter of millimetres in size. The second category of "filled pasta" breaks down into ravioli, tordelli, tortellini and agnolotti. For commercially produced pastas, you can choose from your preferred brands of spaghetti, farfalle, fusilli, maccheroni, penne, rigatoni and many more.

Once upon a time pasta making was limited to a few shapes, such as tagliatelle and tagliolini, which get their name from the Italian verb "tagliare" – to cut. Before the mechanical pasta-making machine was invented, the only way was to smooth it out into a soft sheet and then to cut it by hand into more or less pliable strips. Spaghetti, on the other hand, is descended from wire-drawing, done with a mechanical machine. Back in the 17th century, artisans in Genoa, Rome, Naples and Palermo joined together in pasta corporations, laying down precise rules and rigid disciplines for production. However, pasta was already being referred to in the year 1000 AD in Palermo and Genoa, at a time when the mills

The gardens of the Vatican, Rome

were powered by water, the millstones were of stone and the flour was separated from the bran in sieves shaken by hand. This procedure is still used in some mountain areas, producing exquisite flours. In 1904, the pasta industry was employing nearly 3000 people at Torre Annunziata in the province of Naples, today the centre of excellence for the production of durum wheat pastas, and ships used to leave the port of Naples packed tight with spaghetti and maccheroni.

For impeccable pasta cooking, or as the experts say, for perfect "expression", use the following technique step by step:

- bring plenty of water to the boil in a large pan
- add salt (10gr per litre)
- drop in the pasta (carefully, if it's fresh pasta)
- mix thoroughly for the first 5 minutes to avoid the pasta clogging and sticking
- when cooking time is completed (shorter for fresh pasta), which you will generally find on the pasta packet, pour in a glass of cold water to stop the process and then drain the pasta using a colander
- shake the pasta up in a dish with the sauce (sometimes it is better to season it directly on a large plate which you have previously heated up with a little boiling water or in the oven)
- arrange in portions and serve

The Street Market, Sorrento

Fresh Tomato and Basil Spaghetti
Spaghetti pomodoro fresco e basilico

Spaghetti with tomatoes is the very essence of Mediterranean food. This is a quick recipe which depends on the quality of the ingredients, namely the pasta, of durum wheat without fail, extra virgin olive oil and basil. Think of the sun and the Italian "tricolour" when you make it, because that is what the dish will look like: white, red and green.

**400 gr spaghetti   300 gr tomatoes or Pachino cherry tomatoes
A clove of garlic   A small tuft of fresh basil   Salt, pepper and extra virgin olive oil**

If you have Pachino cherry tomatoes, cook them whole, sauté-ing them in extra virgin olive oil together with the crushed clove of garlic. Close the pan with the lid and allow to cook, stirring now and again. They will be ready after 10 minutes. Dust with shreds of basil leaf. Meanwhile cook the spaghetti, drain and place it in the pan to mix it well with the sauce. Serve in a large, generous dish at the centre of the table, decorating it with a whole leaf of basil. Whole tomatoes should be peeled and diced. Sauté them in the same way and season as indicated above. The whole dish will be improved with a sprinkling of grated pecorino or reggio parmesan.

Maltagliati with Beans
Maltagliati con fagioli

Maltagliati with beans is a typical country dish from Piedmont. It is usually served warm and without grated cheese but it can also be eaten cold and country people will tuck into maltagliati at any time of day… it's irresistible. The pasta and beans are rich in vegetable protein and carbohydrates. I always prepare them in winter for my husband and for the workers who spend whole days amongst the vines out in the cold cutting back the shoots.

250 gr borlotti beans (fresh or dried)   1 small onion
1 sprig of rosemary   400 gr maltagliati (or tagliatelle)
A rasher of cotica (pork skin with a layer of fat) or pancetta
Salt and pepper and extra virgin olive oil

Soak the beans for 12 hours in water. This softening is unnecessary if fresh ones are used. In a pan mash the onion in some extra virgin olive oil and add the fresh beans or the well drained dried ones. Stir and add just enough cold water to cover them completely. Simmer on a low heat for at least one hour. When nearly ready, add pork cotica or pancetta. Then bring to the boil and add the maltagliati, which will cook in a few minutes. Warm up a little extra virgin olive oil on the heat with the rosemary (finely chopped). Add to the beans and serve in a fine earthenware dish.

The Honeymoon Couple, Venice

Trenette with Pesto
Trenette al pesto

On a mention of pesto, thoughts turn to Liguria. This beautiful tongue of land facing the Tyrrhenian Sea smells of basil. Christopher Columbus left from Genoa to discover the Americas, undoubtedly with a jar of basil in a little garden on the poop deck.

400 gr trenette (or noodles)   50 gr fresh basil leaves
4 cloves of garlic (best of all pink garlic)
1 potato or a good handful of broad beans boiled   100 gr pine nuts
50 gr grated reggio parmesan or pecorino cheese   Salt and extra virgin olive oil

Use a fine pink garlic if possible; white garlic is less delicate. Crush 4 cloves and place them in a food mixer. Wash the basil and dry well, cutting the leaves into small pieces and adding them to the garlic. Then add the pine nuts, the grated cheese and the boiled potato or the boiled broad beans, cut into pieces. Then, a good glass of extra virgin olive oil and salt. Mix everything. If the ingredients look as if they need oil, don't worry, add as much as you like, the pesto should end up soft and paste-like: the ingredients used tend to absorb a great deal of oil. The pesto can be kept in a glass jar, covered with oil, for a week. It is better not to freeze it. Season the cooked trenette with the pesto in a dish of generous proportions at the centre of the table.

Tagliatelle with Bologna Sauce
Tagliatelle al ragù bolognese

In Bologna, no home is ever without tagliatelle. They must be light and golden, able to absorb the sauce easily. The secret is in the eggs. If they come from free-range hens they are drier and more are needed for the pasta, but the tagliatelle are nice and yellow. Consequently, for the best tagliatelle, you must go to market to buy eggs or directly from the farm.

400 gr tagliatelle   300 gr chopped tomatoes   150 gr minced pork
100 gr minced veal   100 gr minced chicken breast   50 gr dry red wine
30 gr butter   A stick of celery   A carrot   A small onion
Grated reggio parmesan   Salt, pepper and extra virgin olive oil

Finely chop the vegetables and fry in extra virgin olive oil and butter very slowly until nicely brown. Then add the three types of meat, with salt and pepper to taste. Cook for several minutes and add the wine, which should evaporate completely. Add in the tomatoes, continuing to cook until the meat is well done, with a lid on. Stir frequently with a wooden spoon. When the sauce is ready, boil the tagliatelle and drain off when it is al dente. Add the tagliatelle to the sauce and season it in a large pan stirring well. Serve on a generously dimensioned plate at the centre of the table, sprinkling it with plenty of grated reggio parmesan.

A Terrace in Bordighera

Fettuccine with Mushrooms
Fettuccine con i funghi

Fettuccine with mushrooms are most associated with mountainous areas rather than the plains or coast. The country is crossed by two mountain chains, the Alps and the Appenines, from east to west and north to south respectively and so… it's full of mushrooms! Never wash mushrooms; they should be cleaned only with damp paper, removing the residues of earth and leaves.

400 gr fettuccine   250 gr mushrooms
Chopped parsley   1 large tomato (sliced)
1 clove of garlic (crushed)   1 small onion (chopped)
Salt, pepper and extra virgin olive oil. Butter

Soften the crushed garlic and chopped onion in a little olive oil and butter. Then add the stalks of the mushrooms, the sliced tomato and half of the chopped parsley. Season with salt and pepper. Then add the mushroom caps cut into small pieces. Replace the lid. The sauce will be ready in 10 minutes. Cook the fettuccine, drain and add to the sauce in the pan. Stir well and, if necessary, add a dash of extra virgin olive oil. Serve on individual plates, decorated with a sprig of parsley.

Maltagliati with Borage and Speck
Maltagliati alla borragine e spek

Borage is an aromatic herb which in Italy grows and flowers throughout the year. It is found in fields and along the roadside and it grows on a fleshy stem with rather prickly leaves, producing a small delicate star-shaped flower which pasticcerias use sugared to decorate cakes and to make old-style sweets that children love. If you have a little speck in the house, a kind of seasoned meat similar to bacon, typical of Trentino Alto Adige and Austria, you can prepare this unusual, savoury dish.

400 gr fresh maltagliati pasta   200 gr borage
200 gr diced speck (dry salted meat) or well-dried bacon
Salt, pepper and extra virgin olive oil

Finely chop and simmer the borage in boiling water. Drain and then, in a frying pan, scald it in extra virgin olive oil, adding the diced speck (or bacon). If necessary, mix in a spoonful or two of hot water. When the ingredients are well mixed, season with salt and pepper. Remove from the heat and cover. In the meantime, cook the maltagliati and drain well. Add the sauce to the pasta and put back on the heat. Mix well to tie the sauce to the pasta and borage and serve on individual plates. You can add grated cheese at will and a few small borage flowers for decoration.

Green Lasagne with a Meat Sauce
Lasagne verdi al sugo di carne

Historically, this sauce requires lengthy cooking, which is why the restaurants and rural homes in Emilia allow it to simmer on the wood stove for as much as a couple of hours. On a modern cooker, you can happily make do with average cooking of 45 minutes

**400 gr green lasagne   150 gr minced beef   A small onion   A stick of celery
1 carrot   A cup of tomato sauce   150 gr minced pork
100 gr reggio parmesan   Butter, flour and milk to prepare the white sauce
Salt, pepper and extra virgin olive oil, butter**

Finely chop the vegetables and lightly fry in extra virgin olive oil, together with the minced meat, the tomato sauce, the salt and pepper. Stir frequently. Meanwhile prepare approx 150 grams of white sauce. When the meat sauce is ready, cook the lasagne in plenty of salted, boiling water. Drain off and place the sheets on a linen cloth. Place a layer of the sauce, topped by the white creamed sauce, in a buttered oven dish. Cover with a layer of lasagne and so continue until all the ingredients have been used. Cover with white cream sauce and some flakes of butter. Then cook in the oven at medium heat at a temperature of approx. 160º for about 20 minutes until the surface is golden. Serve in the oven dish at the table.

Tagliolini with Walnuts
Tagliolini alle noci

This recipe is used after the nuts have been harvested, which is done in autumn. Crack the walnuts and reduce the kernels to small pieces. The whole ones can be used as decoration. Walnuts are highly regarded in Italy, the green nuts being used in June to prepare walnut liqueur, which can be kept for years. Use crème fraiche instead of the whipped cream to add a touch of lightness and refinement to this unusual sauce, which can be prepared really quickly if instead of cracking the nuts you use kernels already shelled.

400 gr tagliolini (or tagliatelle)   150 gr shelled walnuts
100 gr crème fraiche   Salt and pepper

Break up the walnut kernels into small pieces and heat gently in a pan with the crème fraiche, mix well and season with salt and pepper. Meanwhile cook the pasta, then add the well drained tagliolini or tagliatelle and stir the whole carefully. Serve on individual plates, decorated with kernels of whole walnuts.

The Grand Canal, Venice

View of Valtournanche and the Alps

Pizzoccheri Valtellina Style
Pizzoccheri della Valtellina

This old recipe from Valtellina comes from the far north of Italy. Valtellina has an excellent tradition of cheeses, and pizzoccheri, which are a combination of buck wheat and white meal, can be admirably married with this vegetarian sauce to produce a delicious rustic dish.

400 gr pizzoccheri (or macaroni)   200 gr greens
2 large potatoes   200 gr soft cheese (they use bitto in Valtellina)
200 gr butter   Salt, pepper and extra virgin olive oil

Boil the potatoes, chopped into pieces, in salted water with the beet leaves, broken up by hand or cut into strips. After a few minutes, add the pizzoccheri to the boiling water as well and cook for around 10 minutes, all together. Drain off. In the meantime, melt the butter in a large frying pan. Then add the pizzoccheri to this with the vegetables and mix. Dice the cheese and add it and serve immediately in a large generously dimensioned plate at the centre of the table. Since pizzoccheri are particularly thick, cooking them with the vegetables will allow them to absorb their full flavour.

Linguine with Cockles
Linguine alla vongole in bianco

Cockles bring the sea to the table and a good sprinkling of ground white pepper brings out the flavour even more. Cockles should be purchased whole, in the shell; I prefer them as they come but in many parts of Italy they add tomato sauce.

400 gr linguine   1 kg of cockles in the shell (or 300 gr shelled)
A glass of dry white wine   3 cloves of garlic   A small bunch of parsley
Salt, pepper and extra virgin olive oil

Wash the cockles in running water and place them in a deep pan. Then add a small quantity of water and a glass of white wine. Replace the lid, bring to the boil and wait until the shellfish open after 10 minutes or so, stirring from time to time. Take off the heat and remove them from the pan into a large bowl. Strain the stock and put it to one side. Using a spoon, remove about half of the cockles from the shells. Then prepare the sauce in a large shallow pan. Lightly fry the crushed garlic in a little oil, then add the cockles, salt and pepper and slowly add the cooking water, with a little chopped parsley. Stir frequently. The sauce will reduce. Cook until the cockles are soft. Meanwhile cook and drain the linguine and pour them into the dish, mix well with the sauce and serve in a generously dimensioned plate, sprinkled with the remainder of the chopped parsley.

Plazza of the Arch of Titus, Rome

Bucatini Amatrice Style
Bucatini all'amatriciana

This type of pasta comes from the town of Amatrice in Latium. Bucatini are large hollow spaghetti which slide away on the plate and are difficult to twist round a fork… It's also a quick pasta whose particular feature is its hollow centre (bucatino). If you can only get spaghetti, take the largest that you can find and, particularly of durum wheat. Pasta from durum wheat absorbs this type of sauce particularly well.

**400 gr bucatini (or spaghetti)   100 gr bacon   350 gr peeled tomatoes
Red pepper   ½ onion   A handful of grated mature pecorino cheese
Salt, pepper and extra virgin olive oil**

Chop the onion and bacon in small slices. Place all in a large pan and fry lightly in extra virgin olive oil, then adding the pepper. When everything is done to a golden brown, remove the ingredients from the pan and place them on a plate. Fry the peeled tomatoes in the pan, in the same oil, mashing them with a fork, for 10 minutes. When ready, add the rest of the sauce, which you have kept to one side, and mix well. Cook the bucatini in plenty of salted water, pour off and tip into the pan with the sauce. Stir well and serve on individual plates sprinkled with plenty of grated pecorino.

Fusilli with Tomato, Olive & Caper sauce
Fusilli con salsa di pomodoro, olive e capperi

The addition of olives and capers gives this pasta all the aroma of the Southern Tyrrhenian Sea. The capers should come ideally from Pantelleria, an island lying between Sicily and Tunisia, which supplies the most flavoursome capers. They are smaller than the others and are preserved in salt. A Pantelleria caper can remain caught between the spirals of the fusillo… quite exquisite!

400 gr fusilli   350 gr tomato sauce   An onion
A handful of black stoned olives   A small handful of capers
A small handful of dried marjoram   Salt, pepper and extra virgin olive oil

Chop the onion very finely and fry very slowly in extra virgin olive oil until golden. Wash the capers in water to remove the salt and then add the capers and olives to the onions. Then add the stoned olives and capers. After a few minutes, pour in the tomato sauce, which must be reduced slowly; stir frequently and allow to cook for at least 30 minutes. Season with salt and pepper. In the meantime, cook the fusilli until al dente, drain and transfer to the dish with the sauce, adding the handful of marjoram. Then mix the ingredients well and serve on large individual plates, with a sprinkling of grated pecorino or dry salted ricotta, if desired.

Tagliolini with Roast Meat Sauce
Tagliolini al sugo di arrosto

Tagliolini are a must in Piedmontese cookery and both country and city housewives jealously guard their family recipes for the best roast meat for tagliolini sauce. This recipe is particularly prepared on festive days. The leftover meat can also be saved for a main course.

**400 gr tagliolini   500 grams mixed meats (veal, pork, rabbit)
2 glasses of white wine   Rosemary   Salt and pepper   Extra virgin olive oil**

Cube the meat and fry the pieces in a small amount of extra virgin olive oil until a deep brown. When the meat begins to turn to gold add the white wine and season with salt and pepper little by little. Stir the pieces of meat with a wooden spoon so they cook uniformly. Add a few sprigs of rosemary. Add a little hot water to keep the meat soft if necessary. When the meat is cooked, remove it from the pan and keep it as a second course (excellent with mashed potatoes). Filter the remaining sauce into the pan (the rosemary needles and the small pieces of meat that become detached during cooking will remain in the strainer). Dress the tagliolini which you have cooked in the meantime, with this sauce. Sprinkle with salt and pepper, if needed, and serve in a large dish which you have previously warmed in the oven or by pouring the hot water from boiling the pasta into it. Do not add grated cheese to this dish.

A villa in Tuscany

Via Marmorata, Rome

Spaghetti alla Carbonara

A story of poor people, the Carbonari of Rome, the workers who carried the coal to the boilers to heat up the ovens, forges and homes. Their breaks for food had to be particularly short, which is why this recipe is a must for people with no time to waste, knocked up simply from spaghetti, garlic, oil and pancetta. Adding eggs makes this dish particularly nutritious and tasty.

400 gr spaghetti   80 gr pancetta
A clove of garlic   3 eggs
70 gr grated reggio parmesan
Salt, pepper and extra virgin olive oil

Crush the garlic and fry in olive oil in a large pan. The garlic serves only to give an aroma to the oil so remove it when it turns brown. Add the pancetta and sear. Remove from the heat. In the meantime, cook the spaghetti and beat the eggs with the grated cheese. Then drain off the pasta and tip into the pan, together with the beaten egg mixture and replace on the heat for a few moments. Mix everything well and adjust the salt. Then serve in individual heated plates, with a dusting of grated cheese.

Pasta Timbale with Pasta Rings
Timballo di pasta con anelletti

My husband Saverio, makes a splendid timbale of pasta rings. This is best placed at the centre of the table and is one of the most typical recipes of Southern Italy. Caciocavallo is a traditional Sicilian cows' milk cheese.

**300 gr pasta rings (or macaroni)   350 gr minced beef   250 gr peeled tomatoes
A glass of red wine   1 onion   100 gr Caciocavallo (or Emmental)
Salt, pepper and extra virgin olive oil   Butter**

Finely chop the onion and lightly fry in the extra virgin olive oil in a heavy bottomed casserole dish. Add the minced meat and cook till dark brown. Add the red wine and allow it to evaporate. Finally place the peeled tomatoes, whole and well seasoned, in the casserole. Replace the lid on the pot and allow to simmer. Stir now and again, lowering the flame and allowing to cook for at least 40 minutes. The liquid from the tomatoes will greatly diminish and the meat will take on a fine chestnut colour. Meanwhile cook the pasta rings, drain off when half cooked and keep warm. Butter an oven dish, a round glass one if possible, and prepare the timbale. Pour in a layer of pasta rings, one of sauce, and one of Caciocavallo slices. Then build up a second layer of pasta rings in the same way. Cover with Caciocavallo and flakes of butter. Bake in a hot oven at 180° for 10 minutes and serve at table with a ladle.

Lake Maggiore from Isola Bella, Lombardy

Spaghetti with Seafood
Spaghetti ai frutti di mare

Italy is a peninsula where people have always lived from coastal fishing and Mediterranean seafood is particularly flavoursome. If it comes from other seas, you have to be generous with the white wine and parsley to achieve the additional taste that the high salinity of the Mare Nostrum (as the ancient Romans called it) gives to our fish. Spaghetti and linguine are the ideal pasta for fish and if possible, use durum wheat pasta, as it absorbs the sauce better. We do not advise adding anchovies to the sauce; do so only if your seafood seems altogether too insipid. Fishermen used to prepare this sauce with the leftovers from the sale of their fish; a few mussels, a few cockles and other shellfish. Add a little garlic and tomato and your meal is made. Simple recipes are the key to Italian cookery. Forget spices and stock-cubes; they're out of place and do not add anything to your pasta.

**350 gr spaghetti or linguine   300 gr small mussels in the shell
300 gr cockles in the shell   300 gr fasolari (large mussels) in the shell
A handful of fresh parsley   2 tomatoes
4 cloves of garlic   A glass of white wine
Salt, pepper and extra virgin olive oil**

Wash the seafood well under running water and remove the beards from the mussels. Pour all into a large casserole and add a good glass of water and one of dry white wine. Replace the lid and leave it until the shells open. (Place the fasolari at the bottom of the dish as they are bigger.) Stir a couple of times and take off the flame when all the shells are open. Then separate half of the seafood from their shells, using a teaspoon. Strain the stock and leave it to one side. Lightly fry the crushed garlic in oil in a large pan, adding the fresh tomatoes quartered and the chopped parsley. Salt and pepper plentifully. Add the seafood with and without shells, stir and add the stock which you have just filtered. The seafood should continue to cook in its juice, also additionally acquiring the flavour of the tomato. If required, you can add a little pimento according to taste. Cook the pasta, drain off when half cooked and pour into the dish with the sauce, then cook until ready. The stock will then be nicely absorbed. If the sauce tends to dry up during cooking, add a spoonful of water and one of dry white wine. If you do not have enough liquid to finish cooking the pasta, add a ladle of water from boiling the pasta. Serve on a large generously sized dish at the centre of the table, adding a dash of extra virgin olive oil and the remainder of the chopped parsley.

Farfalle with Courgettes and Prawns
Farfalle zucchini e gamberetti

This pasta is a happy combination of ingredients from land and sea. The courgettes marry perfectly with prawns, by nature soft and delicate, providing a mix of colours from pink to green; good to look at and good to taste. To make it more flavoursome, add a short fish-head bouillon as a highlight which will tilt the balance more towards the seafood than to the land food.

**400 gr farfalle   200 gr shelled prawns
A fine fish-head (sea scorpion, sea perch, etc)   300 gr courgettes
Salt, pepper and extra virgin olive oil   Fresh chopped parsley**

Place the fish-head in a pan with a little water and white wine, season and replace the lid. Cook for 10 minutes. Take off the heat and filter the stock. Then carefully clean the head, retaining all the little pieces that you can gather. You should throw away only the skeleton of the head and the eyes. Replace the fish pieces on the heat in the filtered stock and add the prawns, which will cook in a few minutes, especially if shelled. In another pan, lightly fry the zucchini in a little oil, cut into roundels, adding a little hot water. Mix the two sauces together. Cook the linguine al dente, drain off and pour out into a sizeable dish. Place at the centre of the table, sprinkling with chopped parsley.

Fishermen in the Bay of Naples

Penne Norma Style
Penne alla Norma

This dish was dedicated to the opening night of Norma, the lyric opera by Vincenzo Bellini, by various Sicilian restaurants. This is one in the Catania style, the home town of the composer.

**1 onion   400 gr penne   300 gr tomato paste   300 gr aubergine
100 gr salted ricotta   A sprig of basil   Salt and extra virgin olive oil**

Mix the ingredients cold, adding the finely chopped onion, oil, salt and pepper to the tomato paste. Then cook for around 30 minutes. The tomato should reduce by half. Chop and fry the aubergine. Cook the penne in plenty of salted water, drain off and pour into a pan together with the sauce. Then add the salted ricotta and flavour it with the basil leaves. Stir well to mix the whole and serve on individual plates, adding a few leaves of aubergine and some freshly grated salted ricotta. If you cannot find fresh salted ricotta from the South of Italy, use fresh goat cheese seasoned with salt and pepper. You should in that case use less of the final gratings on the individual plates. You can decorate with fresh basil leaves.

Rigatoni Trapani Style
Rigatoni alla Trapanese

This is a pasta recipe with a cold sauce; the pasta is cooked separately. If you have been to Trapani you will know why because this corner of Sicily facing the Tyrrhenian Sea a few sea miles from Tunisia, gets really hot. The sea is crystalline and the south wind carries away the sweet smell of Marsala wine as it ferments in the vats. The Stagnone area of Trapani boasts Italy's best saltings and the "flowers of salt", delicate and spicy, best suited for salt-and-pepper dressings and piquant sauces for summer pastas, are found at the centre of the heaps of salt left to dry in the sun.

400 gr rigatoni   2 very ripe salad tomatoes
A good handful of basil   200 gr shelled and roasted almonds
Salt, pepper and extra virgin olive oil

Peel the tomatoes, and cut them into small pieces. Mash the flesh with a fork in a large dish. Add the basil freely, finely chopped. Sprinkle with salt and pepper and mix thoroughly. In the meantime roast the almonds in the oven under a moderate heat. Crumble or whisk them into small pieces, but not too small. Cook the rigatoni in plenty of salted water, drain off and pour them into the dish with the sauce. Stir, adding the crumbled almonds and serve on individual plates. Decorate with whole roasted almonds.

Wild flowers in the Alps

Farfalle with Lemon and Saffron
Farfalle limone e zafferano

This recipe goes back to Sicily's Arab roots. In Sicily, where saffron and citrus fruits are still grown today, pistachio nuts, green or dried, lend that southern touch and add sweetness to a salty dish. There are actually two types of pistachio, one salty, the other fresh and not salty. The former is used as an aperitif, the second to season pasta.

400 gr farfalle   A sachet of powdered saffron or whole pistils
The grated zest of a lemon   A handful of fresh pistachio nuts
A knob of butter   Salt and pepper
A small handful of grated reggio parmesan

Allow the farfalle to cook in plenty of salted water. In the meantime, melt the butter on a high heat in a dish large enough to contain the pasta. Before it gets too hot, add the pistachio nuts (broken into pieces) and, soon after, the grated zest of lemon and saffron. Turn down the heat and, if necessary, thin with a little of the water from cooking the pasta. The sauce will be ready within a few minutes. Drain off the pasta, al dente, and place it in the pan, mixing well. Sprinkle with grated reggio parmesan and serve in a large dish at the centre of the table, decorated with whole pistachio nuts.

Tacconi or Pappardelle in Game Sauce
Tacconi o pappardelle al sugo di cacciagioni

This recipe from Umbria can be adapted to various kinds of game. Umbria is covered with luxuriant woods and the hunting season is always eagerly awaited. In restaurants in the autumn first courses are often served with a game sauce as well as with black truffles. Excellent salamis are also made from wild boar.

To prepare this dish the meat must be well marinaded. For most game this need only be done for about two hours, using wine with a handful of myrtle or juniper berries, bay leaves, pomegranate seeds and sliced apple together with a little extra virgin olive oil and white pepper grains. The marinade should cover the meat and I prefer to use white wine.

350 gr pasta (pappardelle or tacconi)
500 gr game meat (pigeon, pheasant, partridge, hare, etc)
1 large onion   Myrtle or Juniper berries   1 apple
Pomegranate seeds   1 litre wine for marinading
A few bay leaves   Salt, pepper and extra virgin olive oil

Remove the meat from the marinade and dry it. Heat extra virgin olive oil in a high-sided casserole with a cover fitting as tightly as possible. Then fry the meat till brown, turning it well on all sides. If the game has bones, don't worry, the bones will come unstuck from the meat when cooking has finished and can be removed. When the meat is well browned, add the marinade a little at a time. Sprinkle with salt and pepper and cook on a slow heat until the meat becomes soft. This will certainly take a couple of hours. It cooks best when the casserole is tightly covered. Stir now and again and test how well the meat is cooked with the point of a knife. When cooking is finished remove the meat, separate any bones from the flesh and chop all the meat finely. If the marinade runs out during cooking, add fresh white wine. If, on the other hand, there's too much, simply remove a little. Strain the remaining liquid and add the diced flesh to it. Sprinkle with salt (salt should be added only a this point so the meat remains soft throughout cooking). Place everything in a pan for heating up again and allow to stand. In the meantime, you will have prepared the pasta. Pour the pasta and sauce onto a large plate. Stir very carefully with a wooden spoon.

Linguine with Cuttlefish
Linguine alle seppie

Cuttlefish can be served black or white. The cuttlefish ink, found in a bag next to the eyes of this animal and which serves as a defence in the event of attack, is ideal for cooking but it looks a bit risky on a nice table with a white tablecloth. But try it!

**400 gr linguine   500 gr cuttlefish   A sprig of parsley   A glass of white wine
A handful of small Pachino tomatoes   Salt, pepper and extra virgin olive oil**

Put the sac containing the ink to one side. Then cut the cuttlefish into strips. Lightly fry the crushed garlic in oil and add the chopped parsley and the tomatoes (halved). Season well. Add the strips of cuttlefish and cover with the lid. After a few minutes, add the white wine. It must evaporate a little. Cook for around 20 minutes. If you have decided on the black variety, add the ink when cooking has ended. Alternately, if you prefer the white variety, drain off the linguine when half cooked, adding them to the sauce with a little water, if available, from boiling the pasta, and finish cooking them. Serve on individual plates, sprinkling with parsley and flavouring with a dash of extra virgin olive oil undressed. If you prefer black, serve the pasta with its sauce directly on a generously proportioned plate and share out on individual plates.

Figures on a Terrace in Capri

The Italian Riviera at Portofino

Linguine with Courgettes & Almonds
Linguine agli zucchini e mandorle

This recipe has a Sicilian touch and a fresh summer atmosphere. The almond is the first tree to flower in spring and one of the last to shed its fruit at the end of the summer. The almonds, protected in their shells, hang green from the branches as from the end of August, waiting to be harvested. The most delicious pastas are prepared at this time based on roasted almonds, with courgettes from the garden and a leaf or two of fresh mint.

400 gr linguine   200 shelled almonds   500 gr courgettes
A few leaves of mint   Grated reggio parmesan   Salt, pepper and extra virgin olive oil

Slice the courgettes thinly and sauté them quickly in a frying pan with the leaves of mint. Season lightly with salt and pepper. In the meantime, roast the almonds on a moderate heat in the oven, turning them from time to time. When they are ready, crumble them coarsely in a food mixer. Cook and drain the linguine when al dente and tip them into the dish together the courgettes. Then add the crumbled almonds and stir the whole well. Serve on a generously sized plate at the centre of the table with a sprinkling of grated reggio parmesan and a few whole roasted almonds as decoration.

Spaghetti alla Puttanesca

This recipe is taken from popular Roman tradition, based on strong flavours and inexpensive ingredients. There is always plenty of garlic, olives and anchovies in the old quarters of Rome. It would seem that the name of this dish is due more to the combination of ingredients, but, who knows, it could well be that in the 19th century, the more discerning brothels in Trastevere prepared a good dish of spaghetti for the hungry "workers", hence "alla puttanesca" ["harlot style"].

**400 gr spaghetti   300 gr butter   2 spoonfuls of extra virgin olive oil
4 fillets of boned anchovy   150 gr black olives (stoned)
1 spoonful of capers   2 fresh tomatoes (sliced)**

Soak the capers and anchovies to remove the salt, placing both in running water for a minute or two. Then peel the garlic and slice thinly. Heat up the olive oil and the butter in a pan. Then add the anchovies, garlic and capers. The anchovies will dissolve in the heat, encourage this with a fork until a cream is formed. Then combine the stoned olives and sliced tomatoes. Mix well, cooking for several minutes on a strong heat. Then cook the spaghetti and drain off. Tip into the dish with the sauce and mix well. Since the anchovies and capers are salty, I suggest adding salt only to the water for boiling the pasta and not to the sauce. Serve in a fine, generous dish at the centre of the table.

Etna from Taormina

Vegetarian Lasagne
Lasagne vegetariane

I cook vegetarian lasagne in the spring and summer. In summer I add a few broad beans and peas and a good handful of basil. When made with tasty vegetables, this lasagne competes equally with the more famous meat variety.

**400 gr lasagne   100 gr spinach   100 gr broad beans
100 gr potatoes   100 gr peas   200 gr melted butter
Flour, milk and butter for white cream sauce   Grated reggio parmesan
Salt, pepper and extra virgin olive oil**

Chop the potatoes and spinach and boil in plenty of salted water together with the beans and peas. Drain and mix together with the grated cheese, pepper and salt, then add a good spoonful of extra virgin olive oil and the freshly melted butter. Prepare the lasagne; bring it to the boil and when cooked place the sheets on a linen cloth. In the meantime, prepare 150 grams white cream sauce. Place a layer of pasta, covered with the butter and vegetable sauce and then white cream sauce in a buttered oven dish, repeat until the ingredients are used up. Finish with a layer of white cream sauce and flakes of butter. Then place in a moderate oven at approx. 150° for 20 minutes, until the surface has turned golden. Serve the dish at the centre of the table and share out immediately.

Orecchiette from Puglia
Orecchiette Pugliesi

In Puglia orecchiette (literally "little ears") are pasta shapes traditionally made by hand, simply using only durum wheat flour, water and a little salt. They absorb sauces perfectly. Any pasta shapes, such as fusilli, can be substituted.

400 gr orecchiette   400 gr washed and trimmed broccoli
3 salted anchovies   ½ an onion   Salt, pepper and extra virgin olive oil

Bring the water for the pasta to the boil, add salt and pour in the orecchiette. Then, since orecchiette take about 15 minutes to cook, also add the chopped broccoli after 8 minutes, which will be ready in around 8 minutes. Take off the flame. In the meantime, lightly fry the sliced onion in extra virgin olive oil, allowing two spoonfuls of oil per person. Add the anchovies and mash with a fork. Top up with cooking stock and stir. Then drain off the pasta and broccoli and pour everything into a pan. Stir and serve in a large generously sized plate at the centre of the table.

METRIC CONVERSIONS

The weights, measures and oven temperatures used in the preceding recipes can be easily converted to their metric equivalents. The conversions listed below are only approximate, having been rounded up or down as may be appropriate.

Weights

Avoirdupois	Metric
1 oz.	just under 30 grams
4 oz. (¼ lb.)	app. 115 grams
8 oz. (½ lb.)	app. 230 grams
1 lb.	454 grams

Liquid Measures

Imperial	Metric
1 tablespoon (liquid only)	20 millilitres
1 fl. oz.	app. 30 millilitres
1 gill (¼ pt.)	app. 145 millilitres
½ pt.	app. 285 millilitres
1 pt.	app. 570 millilitres
1 qt.	app. 1.140 litres

Oven Temperatures

	°Fahrenheit	Gas Mark	°Celsius
Slow	300	2	150
	325	3	170
Moderate	350	4	180
	375	5	190
	400	6	200
Hot	425	7	220
	450	8	230
	475	9	240

Flour as specified in these recipes refers to plain flour unless otherwise described.